Become the Flowers

Written by
Talia Friedenberg

LICENSING & PRODUCTION INQUIRIES
Uproar Theatrics, LLC.
hello@uproartheatrics.com I www.UproarTheatrics.com

Become the Flowers copyright © 2020 by Talia Friedenberg

Become the Flowers is published by Uproar Theatrics, LLC
500 8th Ave FRNT 3, #1714 New York, NY 10018

ISBN: 978-1-968051-19-8

First Printing, May 2025

SETTING:

A park in the suburbs in spring. Grass, a tree or two, a bench, maybe a swing set or small play structure.

Houses nearby, at least one with a window accessible from the park.

There is a small tent on the grass.

CHARACTERS:

Violet, F, 34 - any ethnicity

Morgan, M, 35 - any ethnicity

Though originally written as 1F + 1M, actors of any gender are invited to explore either character. Names and pronouns should be adjusted as needed.

AUTHOR'S NOTE:

This script is simple, and in real time. It is a quick read. Actors should take their time.

"Vi" is pronounced like "Vy" (not "Vee").

CW: Suicidal ideation.

Lights up on the park. It is eerily silent. Calm? It almost looks like a normal park on a spring day. But the air is dead.

VIOLET, 34, emerges from the tent. She is bundled up and her hair is greasy. She checks her surroundings nervously, then sits on the grass, stretches, and opens a candy bar. She snacks reluctantly. She's hungry and the candy bar is not satisfying. She checks her phone. She doesn't know why — she knows all the cell towers are down. She continues to scan the area. She hums or sings to herself, both out of boredom and as a way to comfort herself. She starts to compose a song, humming and trying out lyrics. She gives up.

A man slowly enters. Violet sees him, and nervously hurries into her tent.

MORGAN, 35, enters. He's carrying a duffel bag. He's been wearing the same clothes for a week at least. He takes in the park. He walks to the swings and sits in one, dropping the duffel beside him. He sees the tent and keeps his distance. He checks his watch, removes a small notebook from his pocket, and writes the time in it, and puts it back in his jacket.

Violet pokes her head out to see what the strange man is doing. Is he dangerous? He becomes aware that someone is looking at him. He turns and they make eye contact. He jumps up and backs away, panicky.

MORGAN

Oh shit. I didn't. Mean to disturb.
Sorry. I'll leave.

He grabs his bag. She knows that voice.

VIOLET
(still in the tent)

Wait!

MORGAN

What?

VIOLET

Are you. Um.

MORGAN

Can you come out of there if you're going to talk to me?

VIOLET

Morgan?

MORGAN

What --? Who's there??

She unzips the tent and emerges cautiously.

Oh my god. Violet?

VIOLET

Hi.

Awkward.

MORGAN

Wow. Hi.

Awkward laughter?

VIOLET

I can't believe... I didn't know you were in town.

MORGAN

Business. In the city. A conference.
I was just supposed to be here for
the weekend, but.

VIOLET

Jesus. You couldn't get a flight back?

MORGAN

I mean. Once the announcement was made, everything pretty
much shut down.

VIOLET

Right.

MORGAN

I, uh, I stayed in my hotel until the riots started, but after that
I figured better get out of the city. Took me almost a week to
get here.

VIOLET

A week?

MORGAN

6 days, 17 hours and...

He checks his watch.

MORGAN (CONT'D)

42 minutes? Ish?

VIOLET

That's...specific.

MORGAN

Just keeping track of time.

VIOLET

How much do we have left?

MORGAN

Have you not been keeping track?!

VIOLET

I don't have a watch and my phone has been glitching out —
how much time do we have left?

MORGAN

If the announcement was completely accurate, it would be...
About 14 hours.

VIOLET

That's it?

MORGAN

That's it.

VIOLET

That's. So soon.

MORGAN

Yeah.

VIOLET

Fuck!

Beat.

MORGAN

Is Eli here?

VIOLET

We got separated during the riots.

MORGAN

Ah.

Beat.

VIOLET

Okay. This is weird.

MORGAN

Very.

VIOLET

I feel like I should. Offer you something. Do you want a bit of this?

MORGAN
(gesturing to his duffel)

I'm fine. I have enough.

VIOLET

Is that... Is it all food?

                    MORGAN
Yeah, do you...?

                    VIOLET
I don't want to take your food. But. I've only had shitty
candy bars for days, and --

            *He opens his bag and tosses her a store-bought
            packaged sandwich.*

Are you sure?

                    MORGAN
14 hours.

            *Violet opens the sandwich package and eats
            eagerly. She moans.*

                 MORGAN (CONT'D)
                    (smiling)
I forgot about your food thing.

                    VIOLET
Sorry. I can't help it. It feels like it's been forever since I had
real food. If you can even call this real food. Thank you.

                    MORGAN
Of course.

            She eats for a moment.

                    VIOLET
So... What have your last two weeks been like?

                    MORGAN
Solitary, I guess?

VIOLET

Yeah? No purge activities? Sex parties? Steal an Aston Martin and see how fast it'll go?

MORGAN

Not particularly? Other than theft. Petty theft.

VIOLET

Right.

MORGAN

And you?

VIOLET

The first week we barricaded ourselves in our apartment. Since we got separated, I've just been trying to stay safe. Heard this area was pretty much deserted and I thought, why not? I had cousins who grew up around here so I kind of know the area from visiting.

MORGAN

I remember.

VIOLET

Oh. Right. I forgot you came with me that time.

MORGAN

Yeah. The tent was a good find.

VIOLET

I actually didn't steal it. We had it at home and I managed to grab it on the way out. We think someone set fire to our building.

MORGAN

People are losing their minds.

VIOLET

Can you blame them?

MORGAN

It's ridiculous that violence is people's first impulse. Like really? It's not like they're fighting for something. They're not making a point, they're just. Destroying for the sake of destroying. It's insane.

VIOLET

They need to put their energy somewhere.

MORGAN

Someone burned down your home! With you inside!

VIOLET

It doesn't really matter, though, does it?

MORGAN

It should!

VIOLET

C'mon, isn't there anything you wanted to try but couldn't before? Something illegal, dangerous?

MORGAN

Sure, who hasn't? But I would never do it. I'm still a rational human being.

VIOLET

What is it? Arson? A big orgy with a bunch of strangers? Hack someone to death with a battle axe?

MORGAN

Jesus Christ.

                    VIOLET
Oh come on, I'm not gonna judge you.

                    MORGAN
I... What would yours be?

                    VIOLET
I asked you first.

                    MORGAN
Fine. I guess, yeah, it would be really cool and satisfying on
some primitive level to just watch something burn.

                    VIOLET
Knew it.

                    MORGAN
Like a skyscraper, or even like an airplane or something, to
light it up and watch it crumble. But now it just seems.
Disrespectful?

                    VIOLET
Yeah.

                    MORGAN
Would you do your thing?

                    VIOLET
I mean, I haven't. So I guess not.

                    MORGAN
What is it?

                    VIOLET
Acid.

MORGAN

Really!

VIOLET

Yeah. I've always wondered what it would be like.

MORGAN

You used to be so against drugs.

VIOLET

I'm not *against* them.

MORGAN

If I handed you some LSD right now would you do it?

VIOLET

I... No. I don't think so. Because what if I have a bad trip and I die terrified?

MORGAN

I mean. I feel like that's not unlikely even without the acid?

VIOLET

Morgan!

MORGAN

Sorry! But I mean...?

VIOLET

You're probably right, but adding drugs to the mix feels a little too risky for me.

MORGAN

Fair enough.

VIOLET

Have you ever done it?

MORGAN

Oh, no. Hallucinogens are not my thing, you know that.

VIOLET

I know that was true in college, but you never know. People change.

MORGAN

I guess.

VIOLET

You don't think you've changed?

MORGAN

In small ways, sure, maybe. But nothing significant.

VIOLET

You still stay up until 4 and wake up at noon?

MORGAN

Sometimes.

VIOLET

I think I've changed.

MORGAN

How so?

VIOLET

Oh, I don't know. I'm married?

MORGAN

Yeah? And?

VIOLET

And I've had to adjust a lot to the industry I'm in. Or, was in. Tours, studios, the physical toll of singing so much, the pressure of composing on someone else's timeline and budget...

MORGAN

And that's changed you? Being married and being a musician?

VIOLET

Yeah? I think so. I'm more... I don't know. I think I've had to adjust more to working around other people's stuff, and collaborating, and just dealing with other people's shit.

MORGAN

That's good.

VIOLET

I don't know if it is. I think it's easy to kinda lose yourself if you're always working around other people.

MORGAN

Maybe. If you take it too far, sure. But it's good to be able to put other people first sometimes. Compromise.

VIOLET

Subtle.

MORGAN

What?

VIOLET

You always accused me of being unwilling to compromise.

MORGAN

Yes, well. No need to dwell on past mistakes.

VIOLET

Even when the compromises you were asking me to make were completely ridiculous.

MORGAN

It wasn't always my choice, Vi, when you're 22 and offered a lead position in a lab you have to take it! Just because it was far away from *you* --

VIOLET

You're right. No need dwelling on past mistakes.

MORGAN

Fine.

Long beat. Morgan marks the time in his notebook again.

VIOLET

I can't believe it's all going to be gone.

MORGAN

Most of it already is.

VIOLET

Yeah, I know. Japan, right?

MORGAN

Yeah, that whole part of the world is probably long gone. Any island nation.

VIOLET

And the Middle East. Whatever was left of that--

MORGAN

Ashes. I mean, all of this is assuming that the announcement
was completely accurate. We don't really have a way of
knowing at this point, but I'd say it's safe to assume.

VIOLET

Where else?

MORGAN

Most of Western Europe and a lot of Asia are underwater by
now. Africa has been ablaze for a while.

VIOLET

Isn't Russia totally wiped out too? I read somewhere it's like
the climate of the moon.

MORGAN

I don't know about that, but regardless, we're some of the
last.

VIOLET

I knew it was coming, we all knew, but people always said it
would be in, like, a while. Like it would happen to our great-
grandkids.

MORGAN

Sure, but also, this is the last big thing, our first-world
Armageddon. We are straight-up lucky to have made it
this far. We already lost millions in other parts of the world.

VIOLET

Yes I know, thank you. I'm not saying I'm surprised, I'm
just.

MORGAN

Yeah.

Beat.

VIOLET
Well, I have to say, this is not how I ever imagined I would.
Spend my last hours -

MORGAN
- Neither did I -

VIOLET
-but. I'm actually kind of glad you're here.

MORGAN
Thanks?

VIOLET
It would have been weird to never seeing you again.

MORGAN
I mean, how long has it been?

VIOLET
A while.

Beat.

Two and a half years.

MORGAN
Your dad's —

VIOLET
— Funeral. Yeah.

MORGAN
Sorry, again, for my behavior that day.

VIOLET

No no, it's fine. He would have been glad you came anyway.

MORGAN

No, it wasn't right. I needed to just be there for you and respect your choices, but I made it about myself and —

VIOLET

Morgan, please. I'm over it. It's fine. I'm just. Glad that's not the very last time I saw you.

MORGAN

So how is Professor Eli? Or. How was he?

VIOLET
(sudden tears)

Was.

MORGAN

Oh god, I'm sorry. I didn't mean.

She takes a beat, trying to pull it together. He can't find any words.

VIOLET

Sometimes it hits me all over again, like it's the first time. It comes in waves.

MORGAN

I have that too. Like you somehow forgot you were on fire, and you look down and realize, oh shit.

VIOLET

I lost him. I just ran. I knew that's what he wanted me to do and what he would have done and it's actually probably what he did. He could easily be alive right now, but. I couldn't look for him, I couldn't stay in the city. And we had said our goodbyes a million times already.

MORGAN
(bitterly)
At least you got a goodbye.

VIOLET

Yeah.

Beat. Violet realizes what he meant.

Who didn't you get to say goodbye to?

MORGAN
My girlfriend. I mean I did, on the phone. But it's not the same.

VIOLET
Oh god. I didn't know you were --

MORGAN

It's new.

VIOLET

What's her name?

MORGAN

Naomi.

VIOLET
Naomi. How did you meet?

                    MORGAN
On an app.

                    VIOLET
You're kidding.

                    MORGAN
Nope. Only person I've even gone on a date with from an
app. Total anomaly. I can't explain it.

                    VIOLET
Wow. How long have you...?

                    MORGAN
We started seeing each other maybe seven months ago? It
was gradual. We just made it official a few weeks ago.

                    VIOLET
Wow. That's awesome. I'm really happy for you. Not that I'm
happy. I mean. God. I'm sorry. That's horrible.

        Beat.

                    MORGAN
She's so awesome. She's in cancer research. Wicked smart.
We're similar in a lot of ways, which was sort of strange at
first.

                    VIOLET
I'm sure.

                    MORGAN
She's so. To the point. I'm actually the more emotional one in
the relationship if you can believe it.

VIOLET

I mean. You were pretty emotional in our relationship.

MORGAN

But you know what I mean. You're just a more emotional person in general.

VIOLET

I don't know if that's true.

MORGAN

It's not a bad thing, I just --

VIOLET

I wear my heart on my sleeve in a way you don't, sure. I can't conceal my emotions as easily. But that doesn't mean I have *more* of them. You were the one calling me crying for weeks after we broke up.

MORGAN

Okay. Sure.

(quickly redirecting)

She's just simple and easygoing in most ways but fun and exciting in all the ways she should be. I was even starting to think we could be the real thing, long term.

VIOLET

I wish I had gotten to meet her.

> *Beat. Morgan checks his watch again. Violet tries to think of something to say. After a long moment,*

MORGAN

So. How's the music?

                    VIOLET
Oh. It's good. Was good. I guess.

                    MORGAN
Weren't you on some late night show?

                    VIOLET
Yeah, last year.

                    MORGAN
Congratulations.

                    VIOLET
Pays the bills. It wasn't exactly my dream to sing backup for
some 19 year old who weighs 95 pounds and does Adderall
in the bathroom before every performance.

                    MORGAN
But still pretty cool?

                    VIOLET
Yeah, of course, Now it feels. I almost want to laugh.

                    MORGAN
Why?

                    VIOLET
I just spent so many years trying so hard to "make it,"
whatever that means, and now it's like. All that stress, and all
that struggle, and I never got where I wanted to be.

                    MORGAN
But you pursued your dream and you did some really
awesome things. Even if it didn't work out exactly as you
planned.

VIOLET

Yeah. And I guess I'm glad I did it. I would have regretted it
if I hadn't, but still, I really never did anything with my life,
did I? Other than wait around? I can't shake the feeling that I
just wasted so much time, that it was all pointless.

MORGAN

Yeah. I get that feeling too.

Violet looks at him incredulously.

What?

VIOLET

You? You were making medicine for sick people -- that's
actually important.

MORGAN

In the face of all this, no, not particularly, it isn't.

VIOLET

How can you say that?

MORGAN

I'm a scientist, Vi. I chose not to work in the environmental
field. I had the choice and I chose not to.

VIOLET

Morgan, come on, that is not —

MORGAN

All the smartest people I knew, we all rolled our eyes at it.
If we had pooled our resources, really worked together using
our different specializations, maybe we could have done
something! I mean, we never could have stopped it without

MORGAN (CONT'D)
government intervention, but we could have maybe at least
gotten ourselves ready—

VIOLET
You can't put that on yourself. You did important work that
improved people's quality of life while they were alive,
while I did jack shit. This isn't your responsibility.

MORGAN
It was everyone's fucking responsibility.

Beat.

VIOLET
Serves us right?

MORGAN
It certainly does.

VIOLET
Isn't it weird how it polarized though? Like half the world is
burning. It's so far removed from our reality. I can't even
imagine that.

MORGAN
"Some say the world will end in fire,
Some say in ice.
From what I've tasted of desire
I hold with those who favor fire.
But if I had to perish twice,
I think I know of hate
To say that for destruction ice
Is also great And would suffice."

                    VIOLET
Wow

                    MORGAN
What would Frost say now?

                    VIOLET
                    (smiling)
I forgot how much you love to do that.

                    MORGAN
Do what?

                    VIOLET
Quote pretentious shit and hope nobody will get the
reference so you can explain it.

                    MORGAN
I don't do that!

                    VIOLET
Oh my god, yes you do. Or you did, anyway.

                    MORGAN
It's not pretentious --

                    VIOLET
It's fine! You can be pretentious!
It's who you are!

                    MORGAN
Whatever.

VIOLET

Oh don't get butthurt. It's true, and it's okay because you usually are the smartest person in the room anyway.

MORGAN

Great. Good thing Eli's not here to hear you say that.

VIOLET

Why?

MORGAN

I just think he might object. He's not exactly my biggest fan.

VIOLET
(mostly to herself)
And who'd fault is that?

MORGAN

He hated me from the moment he met me. He couldn't handle the fact that you were friends with your ex--

VIOLET
(smiling, lightly)
No no no, this was all you, my friend. You couldn't handle it. You never gave him a chance.

MORGAN

Yes, well. Not all of us had the fortune of falling directly from one relationship into another. Some people have to actually work to make that happen.

VIOLET

And clearly you were working so hard all those years.

MORGAN
(almost giving in to his anger)

Regardless, I think we both know that we never could have been friends. Not really.

Small beat.

VIOLET
(almost smiling)
We were such a mess.

MORGAN
Yup. It's weird to look back on, now that I know what it's supposed to feel like.

VIOLET
What what's supposed to feel like?

MORGAN
An adult relationship.

VIOLET
Oh, yeah. It really did feel like an adult relationship at the time, though, didn't it? With everything that happened. At what, 19 and 20? Just kids. I have to remind myself of that sometimes.

Beat.

MORGAN
How did you go straight from me to him?

VIOLET
(not this again)
What?

MORGAN

It took me years to find Naomi and figure this out, but you
went straight from the chaos of us to a relationship that's
lasted, what, 11 years now?

VIOLET

Yeah, 11. Yeah. I don't know. It was just such a relief. To not
be anxious all the time and to feel like he brought out the
best in me when I was used to feeling like the bad guy.
You used to tell me I was high maintenance and he never,
ever made me feel like that.

MORGAN

You were high maintenance.

VIOLET

Well. You made me ask for things nobody should have to ask
for.

Beat.

Point is, you and I were incompatible, or at least, we couldn't
be healthy. Eli made me feel healthy. It was that easy.

MORGAN

Wow.

VIOLET

What?

MORGAN

No, I just. I spent years, just, struggling to understand how
you could do that, move on so fast.

VIOLET

I know. I tried to explain so many times, Morgan. Over and over again. That it wasn't about you, and I did not cheat on you, and --

MORGAN
(slowly)
I know. But I get it now. I really do. I'll admit, it still stings when I really think about what happened, but. I think I understand why you did what you did. If you and Eli had what Naomi and I have. I guess can't blame you for making that call. Even if it sucked for me. And it did suck for me, but. I get it.

Beat.

VIOLET

That means a lot to me.

MORGAN

Why?

VIOLET
(slowly, begrudgingly)
It was hard to know that I was, like. The villain in someone's story. Especially someone I cared about. It's hard for me not to carry that around.

MORGAN

Well, there's one small thing we can go to our graves feeling a little better about.

They smile sadly.

VIOLET

Ohhhh. I could use a drink. Got anything in that bag?

MORGAN

Sadly, no. I have a caffeinated soda?

VIOLET

There's gotta be some in these houses.

MORGAN

Probably.

VIOLET

And nobody seems to be home...

They look at each other.

MORGAN

Be my guest.

VIOLET

You think I won't?

MORGAN

Hey, I won't stop you.

> *She finds a rock, gives him a look, approaches a house, and breaks a window. She peaks her head inside.*

VIOLET

There's nobody home.

> *She climbs inside. Morgan shakes his head and checks his watch. Violet quickly returns with a bottle of hard liquor.*

> VIOLET (CONT'D)

Success!

> MORGAN

Maybe you have changed!

> *They sit together. Violet opens the bottle and*
> *takes a swig. They pass it back and forth during*
> *the following dialogue.*

> MORGAN (CONT'D)
> (cringing)

That's good.

> VIOLET

It's awful.

> MORGAN

Oh yeah baby.

> VIOLET

What are you smiling at?

> MORGAN

Do you remember senior year when we got that cabin?

> VIOLET

How could I forget?

> MORGAN

A memorable occasion.

> VIOLET

God, I was freezing. We were drunk the whole weekend just
trying to stay warm.

MORGAN

Actually alcohol is a depressant, so even though it often makes you feel warmer, it actually lowers your body temperature.

VIOLET

Jesus Christ, take a day off, would you?

MORGAN

We did more than just drink, if memory serves.

VIOLET

We certainly did. I think I had some trouble walking for a few days after that.

MORGAN

Sorry...?

VIOLET

We did pretty good together.

MORGAN
(correcting her)

Well. Pretty well.

She gives him a look.

We were, though. Good.

VIOLET

We had some...adventures.

MORGAN

Yeah.

Beat. Lingering eye contact.

                    VIOLET
We're not going to have sex.

                    MORGAN
Did I ask you to have sex?

                    VIOLET
No.

                    MORGAN
Okay?

                    VIOLET
Just making sure.

                    MORGAN
Okay.

                    VIOLET
Good.

            Painfully uncomfortable beat.

                    MORGAN
Why did you say that?

                    VIOLET
Because! I'm just. Realizing I've only been with two people
in my whole life? And Eli is wonderful and he's the love of
my life and the best sex I've ever had. But. When I tell
stories about the wildest things I've done, they're with you.
But that does not mean we're going to have sex, even if the
world is ending.

                    MORGAN
Got it.

                          VIOLET
That's all.

                          MORGAN
Do you regret not doing more adventurous stuff? Or being
with people?

                          VIOLET
                    (thinking for a second)
No? I mean, I don't know. Part of me does regret it. But I
made the best decisions with the information I had at the
time, so.

                          MORGAN
That's good.

                          VIOLET
Were you with a lot of people?

                          MORGAN
More than you.

                          VIOLET
I'm sure you have some stories.

                          MORGAN
I do. But I'm not going to tell them
to you.

                    She smiles and swigs from the bottle. Morgan
                    checks his watch, notes the time in his notebook.
                    Again.

                          VIOLET
Can you give that a rest?

MORGAN

No. Problem?

VIOLET

Do you realize how morbid that is?

MORGAN

Morbid?

VIOLET

You're just. Counting down to your own death.

MORGAN

It's calming me down. Forgive me for finding a way to feel
some semblance of control over this. A coping mechanism. I
can't stop it or change it or call my girlfriend or do
absolutely anything to feel anything other than completely
useless and hopeless. I know it's irrational, I can assure you I
see the irony in something so irrational being the thing that's
calming me down, but it's how I'm getting through this, so
please leave me alone.

VIOLET

Okay. Sorry.

MORGAN

It's fine.

Violet turns to the tree and rises slowly.

VIOLET

There's something. Do you hear that?

*She moves towards the tree. Morgan rises
abruptly.*

MORGAN

No, what is it?

> *Something falls out of the tree and they jumps back. She creeps back to inspect, Morgan right behind her.*

VIOLET

What is that?

MORGAN

It's a baby bird?

> *It's a very young blue jay chick. Young enough that it's not cute yet. It's maybe even a little gross.*

> *They're both a little panicked, especially Violet.*

VIOLET

God, shit. It's dying.

MORGAN

Should we. Help it? Or kill it?

VIOLET

Oh, I don't want to kill it. But. Maybe?

MORGAN

It'll happen anyway.

VIOLET

Right, so why should we do it?

MORGAN

It's humane? Maybe?

VIOLET

We can't touch it, it could be diseased...

> *They look at each other. It doesn't matter if the bird is diseased, does it?*

> *Violet hesitantly picks up the dying bird and sits, holding it to her stomach. It might make pitiful sounds. Morgan sits with her.*

> *Violet is still panicking, but calms herself as she tries to calm the bird.*

VIOLET (CONT'D)

Okay. Okay. It's alright. You're warm now. I'm sorry you're in pain. I wish there was something I could do. But I can hold you and keep you warm. I hope I'm not scaring you and that you feel safe. At least.... Don't be scared.

MORGAN

Fuck.

VIOLET

Do you want to hold it?

MORGAN

No.

> *She extends the bird to him. He shakes his head, barely able to look at it. She nods and holds the bird close to her again.*

MORGAN (CONT'D)

Should we feed it?

VIOLET

I don't think so.

She starts to hum or sing to the bird. After a few moments, she stops. The bird has died.

I'm sorry.

She transfers the bird to one hand and starts to paw at the ground with the other.

He helps her hesitantly and they dig a little hole. She looks at the bird again, and gently lowers it into the hole. They look at the shallow grave.

MORGAN

Maybe it's lucky. It missed the worst of it.

VIOLET

Maybe.

MORGAN

This is dumb.

VIOLET

No it isn't.

Together, they cover the bird with dirt. When they're done, Morgan gets up and walks away. Violet stays, with her hands over the mound. He turns and sees her silently (praying?) over the bird.

MORGAN

You would've made a great mom.

Beat. Morgan picks up the alcohol again.

VIOLET

Thank god I'm not though, right? Can you imagine having kids though this? Burying them?

MORGAN

Why didn't you?

VIOLET

Timing. Eli. I don't know anymore.

She rises from the grave.

MORGAN

I'm sorry. I know how much that meant to you and I wish you could have --

VIOLET
(daggers)

Don't.

MORGAN

What?

VIOLET
(flatly)

Shall we retrace all the things we wish we'd done differently now that can't do anything about it?

MORGAN

Right.

She takes the bottle from him and swigs. They continue to pass it back and forth.

VIOLET
(gesturing to grave)
Do you think he's anywhere now? Beyond?

MORGAN
No. He's gone. You know I don't believe in an afterlife.

VIOLET
Yeah. You're probably right.

MORGAN
You agree?

VIOLET
Probably. You....

MORGAN
What?

VIOLET
Sorry. I have to ask. You've seen it.

MORGAN
What?

VIOLET
Death?

MORGAN
(gesturing to the bird grave)
Yeah? So have you.

VIOLET

No, I mean human. I wasn't there when my dad passed. I
missed it.

MORGAN

Oh. I'm sorry.

VIOLET

Me too. That's one of those things.

MORGAN

You, uh. You saw my mom though?

VIOLET

No I didn't. I had gone out to get something at the drugstore.
And you never really told me what happened. And she was
your mom and I didn't want to pry, and I just needed to be
there for you but I guess I was kind of waiting for you to...
And you never did. I thought maybe I had done something,
or I didn't make you feel safe enough. Which sucked, but.
You were the one who just lost their mom so I kept it to
myself.

Short beat.

I was so glad you showed up to my dad's funeral because I
wanted to ask you about her. I had been, sort of, I guess,
channeling you all through those last months with him?
Because you were just so practical and calm. I still don't
know how you did that at 21, so gracefully. And even though
I have no idea what was going through your head at the time,
it was, I don't know, grounding to me, to emulate you. And
you got to be in the room with her and. I didn't understand it
at all, what that was like, I mean, that bird is the most death
I've ever witnessed. And now...

Short beat.

VIOLET (CONT'D)
Anyway. I just wanted to know what it was like to be in that room with your parent. I felt like if you explained it to me it would help me understand. And accept it.

MORGAN
You never said anything.

VIOLET
Well I couldn't exactly ask you when you and Eli were. Being. Boys. I got by without.

She turns to him.

VIOLET (CONT'D)
Will you tell me about it?

MORGAN
(slowly)
It was. Anticlimactic. I was sitting there with my dad watching the news. She was on the machine and a nurse came in and was, I don't know, changing her IV bag or something. And her heart just stopped. People came running in to try to save her, but she had a DNR, so. That was it.

VIOLET
And did. Was there any, like. Her soul leaving her body? Or anything?

MORGAN
No. Her body just couldn't take it anymore. She was in a lot of pain.

                    VIOLET

And that's it.

                    MORGAN

Yes, and I never felt her presence or anything ever again, she
was just gone. That's it.

                    VIOLET

Thank you for telling me.

                    MORGAN

You're welcome. I'm sorry it's not a better story.

                    VIOLET

It's okay. I wanted the truth.

        Beat.

              VIOLET (CONT'D)

I've never forgotten how wonderful she was to me, and to
everyone. Even if you never felt her presence again, she left
an impact. She lived on in all of us, and if there's an afterlife,
that's it.

                    MORGAN

Sure. It's a nice thought, anyway. But you do realize that
nobody will be left to remember us? By that logic, it'll be
like we never existed.

                    VIOLET

Oh. That completely backfired. Sorry.

MORGAN

Don't be. I've never understood the need for afterlife. Even with my mom, even with how horrible that was and how young I was, and how angry it made me, I never felt like some delusion of her not really being gone would help me. I was angry at her doctor, angry that modern medicine wasn't advanced enough to save her. Angry that it happened. But at the end of the day, death is just a thing that happens. It doesn't mean anything other than the thing it is. This is perhaps a more dramatic, biblical version, but it's the logical conclusion to our story. I don't mean to be harsh -- I am as sad and sentimental and angry as the next guy, I just.

He shakes his head.

Who knows, maybe we'll end up in a cloud castle and my mom and your dad will be there and everyone will eat cake and fuck all day and we'll laugh about this. But I'm not betting on it and I don't understand people who do. Our bodies are just a collection of particles and cells that will be absorbed back into the fabric of our ecosystem. If anything, the afterlife is the plants and bacteria that will grow from our decaying bodies. Even if humans and most animals are being wiped off this planet, things will still grow. New life will still begin. Just not ours.

VIOLET

"Lay her in the earth, and from her fair and unpolluted flesh may violets spring."

Beat.

MORGAN

Doesn't get more pretentious than Hamlet...

VIOLET

I memorized that line when we studied it in high school. Her death was just so sad to me. And to have my name be part of it...

Beat.

VIOLET (CONT'D)
(suddenly panicked)

Should we just. Do it?

MORGAN

Do it?

VIOLET

Yeah. Like. End it now. So we go on our own terms?

MORGAN

Oh.

VIOLET

What did you think I meant?

MORGAN

You want to kill yourself?

VIOLET

I don't, I mean, I'm not suicidal I just, I can't stand the idea of drowning, asphyxiating, and those moments of powerlessness, still conscious. I wish I could do it on my own terms.

MORGAN

I mean. How would you do it?

VIOLET

I don't know. I don't suppose you have a gun in that duffel?

MORGAN

No. But I mean. If that's really what you want, I won't stop you?

VIOLET

You won't?

MORGAN

I mean, I'd love the company, but it's your life.

VIOLET

You want to wait it out?

MORGAN

Probably? I think I want to see how it goes down. I get what you mean though. You could hang yourself.

VIOLET

With what?

MORGAN

You could tie clothes together, use some of the tent or the duffel maybe?

VIOLET
(the reality of what it would
entail hits her. too real.)
...I don't think I could really do it. Go through with it.

MORGAN

Why not?

VIOLET

I'm not suicidal? And I wouldn't want to leave you alone.

MORGAN

Your body probably won't even let you if you tried. If you're not really suicidal. You have parts of your brain in place to prevent that.

VIOLET

Yeah.

MORGAN

Okay. Well. Like I said, I'm grateful for the company.

Beat.

VIOLET

Sorry. That was. Dramatic.

MORGAN

I think you can afford a little drama given the circumstances.

VIOLET

Thanks.

It starts to get overcast. Morgan checks his watch and marks the time in his notebook. He checks his watch again.

MORGAN

Oh my god.

VIOLET

What?

He taps his watch, shakes it, takes it off his wrist
and starts pressing buttons.

MORGAN

No no no no no

VIOLET

What??

MORGAN
(getting more and more frantic)
It says 5:28, but it was 5:26 when we got the whiskey, and
that was—

VIOLET

What are you talking about??

MORGAN

My WATCH is BROKEN--

VIOLET
(overlapping)

Shit.

MORGAN

Why did it have to--

VIOLET
(overlapping)

Morgan, it's okay--

He shakes it, hits it, bangs it against a rock.
Then, with a scream, he chucks it as far as he
can away from himself.

MORGAN

FUCK YOU

Beat.

It's hopeless, Violet.

VIOLET

I don't think I can argue with that.

MORGAN

Good. Don't start lying to me now. I'm trying so hard to think of something to do. Something to make this better, bearable, but this is a fucking joke. A JOKE.

> *He sits. Crumbles completely. She hesitantly sits with him.*

> *Long beat.*

VIOLET

What's one thing you're proud of from your life?

MORGAN

What?

VIOLET

Answer the question.

MORGAN

I really don't have the bandwidth.

VIOLET

Just one thing. Come on.

MORGAN
(slowly)
Uh. I don't know. I guess. I ran the lab? And I was damn
good at it. We invented some drugs that slowed
alzheimer's symptoms in patients who showed early signs. It
was so promising, it was going to be huge, and we were
actually pretty close to getting it on the market...

He can't go on.

VIOLET
That is incredible. I know you don't believe in karma, but I
do, and I think you have pretty incredible karma.

MORGAN
Great. Thanks.

VIOLET
I mean it.

MORGAN
So what are you. Proud of?

VIOLET
Oh. Well. It's nothing compared to yours but. My EP?

MORGAN
Your what?

VIOLET
My EP. It was wildly unsuccessful but. I like it. It was honest
and I... I don't know. I thought it was good. I put a lot into
it.

MORGAN

Nice.

He's starting to calm down.

MORGAN (CONT'D)
(slowly)
Tell me something I don't know about you.

VIOLET
(jaw drop)
Oh my god, I completely forgot about that.

MORGAN

Me too, until right now.

VIOLET

We probably wouldn't have gotten together if it weren't for
that game.

MORGAN

Yeah. So?

VIOLET

Oh god, I don't know. Gimme a sec to think. You start.

MORGAN

Typical. Well. I lied earlier.

VIOLET

About what?

MORGAN

My lack of purge activities.

VIOLET

Oh yeah? Impress me.

MORGAN

Right. Well. I finally tried one of the drugs. My drugs.

VIOLET

Oh shit. Had you ever...?

MORGAN

Oh, never. Illegal, big time. I would have lost my job, lost everything.

VIOLET

And?

MORGAN

Honestly? Taking a cognition- enhancing medication when it's like. I had so much mental capacity, and capability, but it ended up just making me feel shitty, because that's not particularly helpful now, you know? When there's nothing to work on?

VIOLET

Yeah. Are you glad you did it?

MORGAN

Sure. I was so curious for so long, might as well.

VIOLET

Yeah.

MORGAN

You go.

Long beat.

VIOLET
I've missed you. I feel like I can say that now.

MORGAN
You missed me.

VIOLET
Sure. Sometimes I'd find myself wishing I could call you to tell you something or share something with you.

MORGAN
I mean. You could have just called.

VIOLET
I know. I could have. But I didn't want it to be misconstrued. And like you said, I didn't know how to be friends with you. Not really.

MORGAN
Yeah.

VIOLET
Your turn.

MORGAN
I got a cat. His name is Winston.

VIOLET
You got Winston Churchill?!

MORGAN

I know it was supposed to be the name of *our* cat, but I really couldn't think of anything better. I didn't know if you'd think it's weird that I took the name so I never told you.

VIOLET

I wish I could meet him.

MORGAN

He's a grouch. He's probably holed up somewhere. I hope he doesn't suffer.

VIOLET

Me too. I'm glad you got him.

Morgan notices that it's raining.

MORGAN

What the-?

VIOLET

What?

MORGAN

The rain.

He rises. She follows.

What time did I say it was? 5:30? We're supposed to have 13 and a half hours left. This isn't right.

VIOLET

The announcement was just an estimation though, right? They can't predict the exact moment the storm hits.

MORGAN

But.

He's speechless. He's panicking.

VIOLET

Wait, I'm sorry. This is it? It's starting?

She holds her hand out to the rain.

VIOLET (CONT'D)
(sincerely)

This drizzle?!?

Morgan laughs loudly.

VIOLET (CONT'D)

What???

MORGAN

"This drizzle??" What did you think would happen?

VIOLET

I don't know! I just wasn't picturing a gentle shower! This is. Pleasant!

They're both laughing now.

Right? Isn't this the most anticlimactic apocalypse you could imagine? Where's the downpour! and thunder and lightning! and whirlwind and tsunamis!

Lightning. Beat. Thunder.

They look at each other.

MORGAN

This is going to be slow, isn't it?

VIOLET

We really just have to sit here and wait until we drown or suffocate or something.

MORGAN

Yup.

VIOLET

I don't know if I can do that. I don't want to die.

He holds her.

MORGAN

Me either.

They just hold each other for a long while as the storm starts to pick up.

They sit.

They calm down. Still holding each other. Still crying.

They look at the sky.

MORGAN (CONT'D)

But hey. How many people get to mourn their own deaths?

VIOLET
(weakly)

Should we eulogize?

MORGAN
(clears throat)
We are gathered here today to - uh -mourn the -

VIOLET
That's how you start a wedding speech, not a funeral.

MORGAN

Oh. Sorry.

Lightning. Short beat. Thunder.

They hold each other tighter.

*They look at each other. They might kiss. Not
passionately, not like "I want you." Just an
expression of some kind of love, some kind of
strange residual intimacy. It means, "I'm not
going anywhere," and "You are still important."*

*But maybe they just hold each other. A squeeze
of the hand.*

The rain really starts to come down now.

They take some deep breaths and look at the sky.

END OF PLAY